Layla ran to her little brother's excited. She pointed to the cale... know what tomorrow morning is?" she asked.

"No, what is it?" said Zayd.

"Tomorrow morning is the first day of Ramadan!" Layla said.

"What's Ramadan?" asked Zayd.

"Ramadan is the ninth month of the Islamic Calendar!" explained Layla.

"I'll see you for Suhoor!" said Layla as she ran out of Zayd's room.

"Time for Suhoor!" said Mom at the dining table.

"What's Suhoor, and why are we eating this early before the sun is even up?" asked Zayd. He was still a little sleepy.

Dad explained, "We eat Suhoor before we start fasting to help us stay strong while we worship Allah during the day."

Zayd thought for a moment. Then he smiled and said, "I can't wait to fast today. I'm so excited!"

"Settle down, class. Today, we will learn what fasting during Ramadan is all about and why Muslims do it," said teacher Amal.

"When Muslims fast during Ramadan, they stop eating and drinking from sunrise to sunset. Muslims also stop doing bad things, like bothering their brothers or sisters or not listening to their parents," the teacher explained.

RINNNNNG... went the bell. The class was over.

Zayd and Layla learned a lot in class!

When they got home, Zayd and Layla rushed to the kitchen where Mom was cooking. They told her what they learned in school.

Zayd said, "Mommy, Muslims fast during Ramadan because Allah tells us to in the Holy Quran, so we can get closer to Allah!"

"Wow! You're right!" said Mom as she grabbed a towel to dry her hands.

"Kids, it's time to read the Holy Quran!" said Dad.

The whole family sat in a circle in the living room. They opened Allah's Book to read Allah's Speech.

Zayd looked at Dad and asked, "Dad, what's the Holy Quran?"

Dad replied, "Son, the Holy Quran is Allah's words, which came down to us in this blessed month long ago. We should read the Holy Quran every day!"

After they finished reading the Holy Quran, Zayd and Layla's stomachs started to rumble.

"I'm hungry!" cried out Zayd.

"Me too, little brother!" said Layla.

Zayd and Layla asked their parents, "Mom and Dad, fasting makes us think about the people who do not have as many things as we do. Can we take some food and clothes to people at the shelter who need them?"

"Sure, that's a great idea!" said Dad. "Ramadan is not just about fasting. It's also about giving to people, helping others, and being good to your parents. Ramadan is about doing as much good as possible, so you can get closer to Allah and make him happy."

When they got home, Mom announced, "Time for Iftar! Now that it's sunset, it's time to break our fast and pray Majrib!"

"The food smells delicious!" said Dad as he grabbed a plate.

"I can't wait to break my fast!" said Zayd.

"Fasting makes me thankful that we have each other, good food, and a nice home to live in!" said Layla.

After eating, Zayd and Dad drove to the Mosque to pray Isha and Taraweeh, together with family, friends, and neighbors.

"Mashallah, the Mosque is so full, Dad! Is this really Allah's House?" asked Zayd excitedly.

"Yes, Zayd, this is one of many of Allah's Houses where Muslims come to think about Allah, pray and thank Him for all He has given us!" answered Dad.

لا اله الا الله محمد رسول الله

At the Masjid, the Imam gave a short talk about how special the last ten days of Ramadan are and how blessed the Night of Power is.

Zayd and Layla looked forward to the Night of Power so they could do extra good and earn many rewards from Allah.

At home, Layla told Mom she wanted to help decorate the house for Eid. Eid is the Islamic holiday that Muslims celebrate after the month of Ramadan ends.

"What a great idea, Layla," said Mom. "The house looks so much better!"

Zayd, Layla, and the whole family went to Grandma and Grandpa's house. Grandpa told everyone about his first Ramadan. Even though fasting during Ramadan may be challenging, he always enjoys it because it brings the family closer!

"You always have the best stories, Grandpa!" said Layla.

When they got home, Layla and Zayd sat and thought about how fasting had helped them do good things, like praying Fajr on time and reading the Holy Quran. They also agreed Ramadan helped them stop what they should not be doing, like sleeping too late and arguing with each other.

When Ramadan ended, Zayd and Layla's family and friends got together for a barbeque and fun in the backyard to celebrate Eid!

"Eid Mubarak to you, Layla! This gift is for you," said Zayd to his sister. He was wearing his new Eid clothes.

"May Allah reward you with good, Zayd! What is this?" asked Layla.

"May Allah reward you with good too, Layla. This gift is a Ramadan board game so we can play it and remember how Ramadan helped us get closer to Allah!" replied Zayd.

"I can't wait until next Ramadan!" said Layla.

The End